Stand Mixer Baking Bootcamp

Transform Your Bakes, From Novice to Ninja with your Stand Mixer

"Conquer your kitchen fears and bake delicious masterpieces with confidence"

Myles Hoover

Table Of Contents

Introduction

Get ready to conquer the world of baking with your trusty stand mixer! This book will be your ultimate guide, taking you from baking basics to impressive showstoppers, all with the help of your powerful kitchen companion.

Part 1: Mastering the Mix

Welcome to the Bootcamp

Before we embark on our delicious adventure, let's get acquainted with the star of the show: your trusty stand mixer! Think of it as your culinary co-pilot, ready to tackle tough doughs, whip up airy meringues, and cream ingredients with effortless grace. Let's unlock its secrets and make these metal muscles your kitchen BFF!

Anatomy of a Powerhouse:

1. Base: Your mixer's sturdy foundation, ensuring stability even when tackling the stickiest of doughs.

Stand mixer base

2. Motor: The hidden hero, pumping out the power to turn those attachments into culinary wizards.

3. Speed Knob: From gentle stirring to high-speed whipping, choose the perfect pace for every task.

4. Tilt-Head and Lift-Bowl Design: Tilt-head models offer easy access to the bowl, while lift-bowl designs provide more stability for heavy doughs.

Stand mixer lift-bowl design

Stand mixer tilt-head

5. Attachment Port: The gateway to a universe of baking possibilities! Here's where you'll connect those magical attachments.

Attachment Arsenal:

Now, let's meet the dream team of attachments that will transform your mixer into a culinary chameleon:

- **Paddle Attachment:** Your go-to for creaming butter and sugar, mixing batters, and blending smooth frostings. Think fluffy cakes and creamy mashed potatoes!

Stand mixer paddle attachment

- **Dough Hook:** This spiral wonder kneads tough doughs for bread, pizza, and pasta with ease, saving your arms from getting a workout. No more tired biceps, just perfectly risen loaves!

Stand mixer dough hook attachment

- **Whisk Attachment:** This airy maestro whips egg whites, cream, and mousses to fluffy perfection. Light meringues, anyone?

Stand mixer whisk attachment

- **Optional Extras:** The fun doesn't stop there! Many mixers offer a plethora of additional attachments, like pasta rollers, meat grinders, and ice cream makers. Get ready to expand your culinary horizons!

Note:

- Consult your mixer's manual for specific instructions and attachment compatibility.

• Don't be afraid to experiment! Mix and match attachments to discover new baking possibilities.

• Keep your attachments clean and dry for optimal performance.

With this newfound knowledge, you and your mixer are ready to tackle any recipe with confidence! Get ready to witness the magic of baking transformed – from messy flour fights to effortless masterpieces, all thanks to your powerful kitchen partner. So, let's plug in, choose your attachment, and get baking!

Mixing Matters

In the grand theater of baking, the humble stand mixer plays the role of a tireless conductor, orchestrating the dance of ingredients into delectable symphonies. But like any conductor, understanding the nuances of movement is key. That's where the science of mixing takes center stage, and knowing how different speeds and techniques affect your culinary creations is crucial to achieving baking bliss.

The Speed Shuffle:

• **Low and Slow:** Think of this as a gentle waltz, perfect for incorporating dry ingredients into wet without over-developing gluten (goodbye tough cookies!). It's also ideal for mixing delicate mousses and whipped cream, ensuring they stay airy and light.

Medium Groove: This is the tango of baking, ideal for creaming butter and sugar until pale and fluffy – the foundation for light and airy cakes. It's also your go-to for mixing batters until just combined, avoiding gluten development that can lead to dense baked goods.

• **High-Speed Hustle:** Picture a disco fever for egg whites and cream! This quick and energetic pace whips them into stiff peaks, perfect for meringues, mousses, and frostings. Be careful though, over-mixing here can turn your fluffy clouds into a grainy mess.

Beyond the Speed Dial:

• **Folding Finesse:** Sometimes, a gentle ballet is needed. Folding dry ingredients into wet batter with a spatula, instead of whipping with the mixer, preserves delicate air pockets for maximum fluffiness. Think soufflés and sponge cakes!

• **Scraping Symphony:** Don't let stray ingredients hide in the corners! Regularly scrape down the sides and bottom of the bowl with a spatula. This ensures everything gets incorporated evenly, leading to smooth textures and no sad streaks of unmixed flour.

• **Temperature Tango:** Ingredients have their own preferred dance moves, too! Cold butter and eggs create denser textures, while room-temperature ones lead to airier results. Let your ingredients come to room temperature for optimum mixing and baking.

Tips for Triumphant Textures:

• **Don't Overmix:** Just like overstaying your welcome at a party, overmixing can be disastrous. Gluten develops with excess mixing, leading to tough bread and dry cakes. Follow recipe instructions and listen to your dough – when it's smooth and cohesive, it's time to stop the music.

• **Start Slow, Finish Strong:** Begin with low speeds to gently incorporate dry ingredients and avoid flour explosions. Gradually increase the tempo as needed, but remember, less is often more when it comes to mixing times.

• **Mix for the Task:** Each recipe has its own ideal mixing style. Follow the specific instructions for best results. Remember, even a waltz can lead to disaster if you try to make soufflé with it!

With these insights into the science of mixing, you'll be a maestro of textures in no time. From melt-in-your-mouth muffins to airy meringues that defy gravity, your stand mixer will become your culinary orchestra, and you, the conductor of deliciousness! So, crank up the mixer, embrace the science, and prepare to be swept away by the magic of mixing!

Remember, baking is a journey of experimentation and discovery. Don't be afraid to adjust techniques, explore different speeds, and find your own rhythm in the kitchen. With practice and these helpful tips, you'll be composing culinary masterpieces that will have everyone singing your praises!

Troubleshooting Techniques

Baking Calamity? Conquering Common Mishaps with Confidence!

Even the most seasoned bakers face occasional kitchen conundrums. But fear not, fellow pastry warriors! We've all been there, staring at a dry cake or dense loaf, wondering where the baking gods went wrong. Well, worry no more! This handy guide equips you with the arsenal to troubleshoot common baking mishaps and transform culinary faux pas into delicious feats.

Dry & Dismal Cakes:
- **Culprit:** Overbaking, overmixing, or inadequate moisture.

- **Fix:** Check your oven temperature – could it be running hot? Did you mix for too long, developing the gluten and robbing the cake of air? Did you forget an ingredient like eggs or oil? Add some moisture with a drizzle of simple syrup or a dollop of sour cream.

Remember, sometimes a slightly underbaked cake is better than a dry one (just do the toothpick test!).

Dense & Dismal Breads:

• **Culprit:** Insufficient kneading, not enough rising time, or incorrect ingredients.

• **Fix:** Did you give your dough a good workout? Kneading develops gluten, giving bread its structure. Let your dough rise to its full potential – did you forget the yeast, or was the environment too cold? Double-check your ingredients – did you accidentally use baking powder instead of bread flour? A little extra love and attention can turn a dense cloud into a fluffy masterpiece.

Curdled & Catastrophic Batter:

• **Culprit:** Temperature clash, overmixing, or acidic ingredients.

• **Fix:** Did you mix cold liquid with room-temperature eggs? Let your ingredients come to room temperature first. Did you get carried away with the mixer? Sometimes, a gentle fold is all it takes. Did you add buttermilk or lemon juice to a batter not designed for it? Try neutralizing the acidity with a pinch of baking soda. Remember, even curdled batter can be salvaged with a little resourcefulness and some extra egg yolks.

Bonus Tips for Baking Bravery:

• **Measure with precision:** A misplaced teaspoon can make all the difference. Invest in good measuring tools and double-check your amounts.

• **Read the recipe carefully:** Don't skip any steps! Baking is a delicate science, and following instructions ensures consistency.

• **Use fresh ingredients:** Quality ingredients lead to quality results. Spoiled eggs or stale flour can sabotage your culinary masterpiece.

• Don't panic! Take a deep breath, assess the situation, and refer to this guide. Most mishaps can be fixed with a little ingenuity and a positive attitude.

Remember, baking is a journey of learning and experimentation. Embrace the occasional mishap as a chance to refine your skills and discover new solutions.

With these troubleshooting tricks and a generous dose of baking bravery, you'll be turning kitchen blunders into baking triumphs in no time! So, preheat your oven, grab your apron, and get ready to conquer the world of baking, one delicious creation at a time!

Part 2: Essential Skills & Drills

Dough Daze No More

Stand mixer kneading dough

Say goodbye to tired arms and hello to perfectly kneaded dough! Your trusty stand mixer is about to become your personal bread-whisperer, transforming shaggy mounds of flour into silky, elastic canvases for culinary masterpieces. Let's ditch the hand-kneading blues and dive into the glorious world of dough-mastery with your mechanical marvel.

Unleashing the Dough Hook:

Forget clunky attachments and flimsy kneading blades. The mighty dough hook is your secret weapon, effortlessly navigating even the stickiest of doughs. But before you plunge headfirst into bread-making bliss, remember: different doughs demand different approaches.

Bread Dough Bonanza:

• **The Lowdown:** Think pillowy loaves and crusty baguettes. Bread dough needs gentle stretching and developing of gluten for that perfect airy crumb.

• **Mixer Maneuvers:** Use the dough hook attachment on low speed, letting it slowly incorporate dry ingredients into wet. Gradually increase speed to medium as the dough comes together. Stop mixing when it becomes smooth and pulls away from the sides, forming a cohesive ball. Remember, overmixing can lead to tough bread, so listen to your dough!

Pizza Perfection:

• **The Lowdown:** Thin and crispy or soft and chewy, pizza dough craves a quick knead for a smooth and pliable texture.

• **Mixer Magic:** Start on low speed with the dough hook, then crank it up to medium for a minute or two. Stop when the dough is smooth and elastic, bouncing back when gently pressed. Speed is your friend here, ensuring a quick knead without overdeveloping the gluten for that perfect pizza crust.

Pastry Panache:

• **The Lowdown:** Flaky croissants, buttery puff pastry, delicate danish dough – these beauties demand a light touch and minimal gluten development.

• **Mixer Finesse:** Use the dough hook on the lowest speed or even pulse mode to barely mix the ingredients. The goal is to incorporate the butter without warming it up, preserving those flaky layers. Stop as soon as the dough comes together in shaggy pieces, then finish the job by hand to avoid overworking it.

Bonus Tips for Dough Domination:

• **Temperature matters:** Use cool or room-temperature ingredients for bread and pizza dough, and keep things cold for pastry dough.

• **Hydration is key:** Adjust the liquid amount based on your flour and desired texture. A wetter dough is easier to knead but requires more careful shaping.

• **Listen to your dough:** It'll tell you when it's ready! Look for a smooth, elastic texture that pulls away from the sides and bounces back gently when poked.

- **Practice makes perfect:** Don't be discouraged by a few rocky batches. Experiment, adjust techniques, and soon you'll be kneading dough like a culinary pro!

With these tips and your trusty stand mixer by your side, you'll soon be wielding dough with the confidence of a master baker. So, preheat your oven, channel your inner bread whisperer, and get ready to create batches of deliciousness that will leave everyone asking, "Did you really conquer your dough daze?" Go forth and bake, dough-mighties!

Butter Me Up

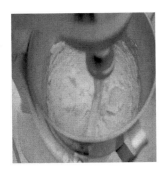

Stand mixer creaming

Ah, creaming butter and sugar – the humble yet essential step in baking that breathes life into your cookies, cakes, and muffins. It's more than just mixing two ingredients; it's a magical transformation, whipping air into the mixture and laying the foundation for light, fluffy textures that melt in your mouth. Let's unlock the secrets of creaming and turn you into a baking maestro who can craft cloud-like creations every time!

Why Creaming Matters:

Think of creaming as aerating. By beating soft butter and sugar together, you incorporate tiny air bubbles that expand during baking, resulting in those irresistible puffy textures we all crave. This fluffy network also traps moisture, keeping your baked goods moist and tender. Skip this crucial step, and you'll be left with dense, disappointing results – definitely not the baking bliss we're after!

The Art of Creaming:

• **Butter Basics:** Start with room-temperature butter, soft enough to easily press with your finger. Cold butter won't incorporate air as well, while melted butter creates greasy textures.

• **Sugar Spiel:** Granulated sugar is your go-to, providing the perfect structure for air bubbles to cling to. For an extra moist crumb, experiment with brown sugar, adding a hint of molasses and deeper flavor.

• **Speed of Light:** Begin at low speed to prevent sugar spraying everywhere. Gradually increase to medium as the mixture lightens and becomes pale yellow. Be careful not to overmix, or you'll lose that precious air and end up with tough cookies.

• **Creamy Clues:** You'll know it's done when the mixture is light and fluffy, with visible air pockets and a pale yellow color. Stop the mixer when it reaches this peak of perfection!

Sweet Twists on the Classic:
• **Brown Sugar Bonanza:** Substitute half or all the granulated sugar with brown sugar for a richer flavor and moisture crumb. Remember, brown sugar adds moisture, so you might need to adjust your liquid ingredients slightly.

• **Shortening Showdown:** Swap some butter for shortening for a higher rise and slightly crispier texture in cookies. Just remember, shortening lacks the richness and flavor of butter, so adjust your recipe accordingly.

Bonus Tips for Buttery Brilliance:
• **Scrape with Scrape!:** Regularly scrape down the sides and bottom of the bowl with a spatula to ensure all the ingredients are incorporated evenly. No stray sugar pockets allowed!

- **Temperature Tango:** Matching ingredient temperatures is key. Room-temperature ingredients cream together smoother and incorporate air more readily.

- **Flavor Fusion:** Add extracts like vanilla, almond, or peppermint for an extra layer of taste sensation. Just blend them in the creaming stage for maximum flavor distribution.

With these butter-creaming secrets in your arsenal, you'll be baking airy masterpieces that will have everyone singing your praises. So, grab your mixer, crank it up, and get ready to transform simple ingredients into fluffy, light delights!

Remember, practice makes perfect, and soon you'll be a creaming connoisseur, wielding your spatula with the grace of a baking guru. Now go forth and butter up the world, one delicious creation at a time!

Whisking Wonders

Stand mixer whisking eggs

Step aside, heavy metal dough hooks and paddle power; it's time to celebrate the delicate dance of the whisk attachment! This nimble dancer of the culinary world whisks away any fear of egg whites and transforms cream into billowy clouds, paving the way for airy meringues, decadent mousses, and angel food cakes that would make angels jealous. So, grab your whisk and prepare to witness the magic of whipped-up wonder!

Conquering Egg Whites:

• **Temperature Tango:** Room-temperature whites whip faster and higher, so let them chill out on the counter for a bit. Cold yolks, however, are your friend – they add stability to the mixture.

• **Separate with Sass:** Avoid yolk contamination, the bane of meringue existence! Use clean, dry bowls and crack shells carefully. A handy eggshell separator can be your yolk-taming ally.

• **Gradual Groove:** Start on low speed to break down the whites, then gradually increase as they become frothy. Patience is key – overmixing leads to a grainy, deflated mess.

• **Stiff Peak Spectacle:** Aim for those luscious, unwavering peaks that stand tall and proud. A gentle fold with a spatula should leave no soft bits behind.

Don't overbeat, or you'll end up with dry, crumbly meringue.

Creamy Cloud Creations:
• **Chill Factor:** Cold cream whips up faster and holds its shape better. So, give that carton a quick fridge visit before you start.

• **Sugar Sweetener:** Granulated sugar adds volume and stability, so sprinkle it in gradually as you whip. Be careful not to overdo it, or your fluffy clouds might turn into a sticky puddle.
Soft or Stiff Peaks? For mousses and frostings, aim for soft peaks that droop slightly when you lift the whisk. For piped decorations, stiff peaks that hold their shape are your goal.

Bonus Tips for Whisking Triumphs:
• **Cleanliness is King (or Queen):** Use grease-free bowls and whisks to ensure maximum air

incorporation. A speck of oil can be the enemy of fluffy peaks.

Acidity Advantage: A pinch of cream of tartar or lemon juice can stabilize egg whites and help them reach even greater heights.

- **Gentle Folding:** When incorporating whipped cream or egg whites into other mixtures, use a light touch with a spatula. Folding preserves those precious air bubbles and keeps your creations airy.

- **Practice Makes Perfect:** Mastering the whisk takes time and patience. Don't be discouraged by a few deflated attempts. Keep whisking, experimenting, and soon you'll be crafting cloud-like masterpieces that will have everyone swooning.

With these whisking wonders in your arsenal, you'll be a master of airy textures and light-as-air creations. So, crank up your mixer, unleash the magic of the whisk, and get ready to conquer the world of whipped-up delight! Remember, a little practice and a lot of enthusiasm go a long way. Now go forth and whisk your way to baking bliss!

Fun Facts

• Dough-n't underestimate the multitasking: Stand mixers aren't just for cakes and cookies. They can tackle heavy bread doughs, light and fluffy meringues, and even shred chicken or vegetables! Swap the whisk for a dough hook, the paddle for a whisk, and unleash your inner kitchen powerhouse.

• Bicep-saving superhero: Ditch the arm workout and let the stand mixer handle the heavy lifting. From kneading bread dough to whipping creamy butter, it takes the strain off your muscles, leaving you free to focus on the fun parts of baking, like decorating those cupcakes with a flourish.

Part 3: Recipe Roundup - From Simple to Sensational

Sweet & Simple

Chocolate chip cookies

Craving homemade treats but short on time or baking expertise? Fear not, friend! Your trusty stand mixer is here to unleash your inner baking diva with Sweet & Simple delights. Ditch the complicated and embrace the easy, because these recipes are designed to tantalize your taste buds without sending you into a flour-dusted frenzy. So, preheat your oven, grab your apron, and let's embark on a journey of effortless baking bliss!

Chocolate Chip Cookie Classics:

1. Creamy Canvas: In your stand mixer fitted with the paddle attachment, beat softened butter and brown sugar until light and fluffy. This is your creamy foundation for chewy cookie bliss!

2. Egg-cellent Addition: One at a time, beat in eggs until fully incorporated. Remember, patience is key – overmixing leads to tough cookies.

3. Flour Power: Add dry ingredients like flour, baking soda, and salt in batches, alternating with milk or vanilla extract. Mix until just combined – a few lumps are okay!

4. Chocolate Chunk Celebration: Fold in a generous heap of chocolate chips (milk, dark, white, or a mix – go wild!). Don't overmix, you want those melty pools of chocolate goodness.

5. Baking Bonanza: Drop spoonfuls of dough onto baking sheets lined with parchment paper. Bake at 375°F (190°C) for 10-12 minutes, or until golden brown and slightly soft in the center. Let them cool on the baking sheet for a few minutes before transferring to a wire rack to fully cool.

Banana Bread Brilliance:

1. Mash Mania: Mash those overripe bananas in a large bowl. The riper, the sweeter and moister your bread will be!

2. Butter & Sugar Symphony: In your stand mixer with the paddle attachment, cream softened butter and sugars (brown and white) until light and fluffy. Remember, this adds air and lightens the texture.

3. Egg-ceptional Addition: One at a time, beat in eggs until fully incorporated. Just like with the cookies, avoid over mixing for a tender crumb.

4. Banana Bonanza: Add the mashed bananas and mix until just combined. You want to see those beautiful banana streaks!

5. Flour Finesse: In batches, add dry ingredients like flour, baking soda, and salt. Mix until just combined – a few lumps are okay, they add rustic charm.

6. Nutty Twists (Optional): Fold in chopped walnuts or pecans for an extra crunch and flavor dimension.

7. Baking Beauty: Pour the batter into a greased loaf pan and bake at 350°F (175°C) for 50-60 minutes, or until a toothpick inserted in the center comes out clean. Let it cool in the pan for 10 minutes before transferring to a wire rack to cool completely.

Vanilla Cupcake Charisma:

1. Creamy Canvas: In your stand mixer with the paddle attachment, cream softened butter and sugar until light and fluffy. This is the foundation for your airy cupcake dreams!

2. Egg-cellent Addition: One at a time, beat in eggs until fully incorporated. Remember, patience is key for that perfect cupcake rise.

3. Vanilla Magic: Stir in vanilla extract for a touch of classic sweetness.

4. Flour Power: In batches, add dry ingredients like flour, baking powder, and salt. Mix until just combined – a few lumps are okay, they add airiness.

5. Milk Maestro: Alternate adding the dry ingredients with milk, mixing until just combined after each addition. Remember, stop mixing once everything is incorporated.

6. Scoop & Smile: Fill cupcake liners two-thirds full with batter. Don't overfill, or your cupcakes might spill over like happy volcanoes!

7. Baking Brilliance: Bake at 350°F (175°C) for 15-20 minutes, or until a toothpick inserted in the center comes out clean. Let them cool in the pan for a few minutes before transferring to a wire rack to cool completely.

Sweet & Simple Bonus Tips:

• **Temperature Tango:** Preheat your oven 15 minutes before baking for consistent results.

- **Measure with Precision:** Accurate measurements are crucial for successful baking. Invest in good measuring cups and spoons.

- **Liner Love:** Use cupcake liners for mess-free baking and easy decorating.
Get Creative: Add sprinkles, frosting, or edible flowers to your cupcakes for personalized flair.

- **Embrace Imperfections:** Not every cookie will be perfectly round or every cupcake a dome of perfection. That's the beauty of baking – enjoy the process and the delicious outcome!

Remember, my friend, these are just the stepping stones on your Sweet & Simple baking journey! With your trusty stand mixer and a sprinkle of creativity, you can whip up endless variations on these classics. Substitute milk chocolate chips for white chocolate and macadamia nuts in your cookies, add mashed strawberries or blueberries to your banana bread, or try swirling your cupcake batter with cocoa powder for a chocolate marble effect. The possibilities are as limitless as your imagination!

So, get ready to unleash your inner baking diva and let the sweet & simple magic of your stand mixer fill your kitchen with the aroma of happiness. With every batch, you'll gain confidence, discover new flavors, and create memories that will be as delicious as the treats themselves.

Happy baking!

Bread Bonanza

Stand mixer making bread

Ready to graduate from simple cookies to crusty masterpieces? Your stand mixer is your gateway to bread-baking royalty! Let's delve into classic beauties like focaccia, sourdough, and braided loaves, mastering the secrets of perfect crusts and airy crumb. Brace yourselves, bakers, for your kitchen is about to become a bread sanctuary!

Focaccia Feast:

1. Hydration Hero: In a large bowl, combine warm water, yeast, and a pinch of sugar. Let stand for 5 minutes until foamy – a sign your yeast is happy and active!

Flour Power: Add olive oil, salt, and most of the flour. Use the dough hook attachment on low speed to mix until a shaggy dough forms. Gradually add more flour if the dough feels too sticky.

2. Knead & Nourish: Increase the mixer speed to medium and knead for 5-7 minutes, or until the dough is smooth and elastic. Add a drizzle of olive oil if needed to prevent sticking.

3. Rise & Shine: Transfer the dough to a greased bowl, cover tightly, and let rise in a warm place for 1-2 hours, or until doubled in size. Punch down the dough to deflate it, then repeat the rising process for another 30 minutes.

4. Olive Oil Oasis: Pour a generous amount of olive oil onto a baking sheet. Gently stretch the dough out onto the pan, dimpling it with your fingertips to create those signature focaccia pockets. Drizzle with more olive oil, sprinkle with flaky sea salt and herbs of your choice (rosemary, thyme, are great options!), and bake at 425°F (220°C) for 20-25 minutes, or until golden brown and crispy. Savor this warm, olive-infused perfection with crusty bites dipped in balsamic vinegar.

Sourdough Saga:

1. Starter Serenade: If you haven't already, nurture your sourdough starter – your tangy, bubbly bread BFF. Then, feed it flour and water a few hours before baking to wake it up from its slumber.

2. Hydration & Flour Fusion: In a large bowl, mix warm water, your activated starter, and a pinch of sugar. Add flour and salt using the dough hook attachment on low speed, incorporating until a shaggy dough forms. Gradually add more flour if the dough feels too sticky.

3. Stretch & Fold Fitness: Embrace the "stretch and fold" technique! Wet your hands, gently stretch the dough out on your work surface, fold it inwards on itself, and turn the bowl. Repeat this folding process every 30 minutes for 3-4 hours, or until the dough becomes tighter and smoother.

4. Shape & Rise: After the final fold, shape the dough into a round boule (ball). Place it in a floured proofing basket (or a well-floured bowl) seam-side up, cover tightly, and let rise for 4-6 hours, or until doubled in size.

5 Baking Brilliance: Preheat your oven with a Dutch oven inside to 450°F (230°C). Carefully transfer the dough to the hot pot, score the top with a sharp knife, and bake with the lid on for 20 minutes. Reduce the heat to 400°F (200°C) and bake with the lid off for another 20-25 minutes, or until golden brown and crusty. Let the sourdough cool

slightly before slicing into its tangy, airy heart –
bread nirvana awaits!

Braided Loaves Bliss:

1. Sweet Dough Symphony: In a large bowl,
combine warmed milk, yeast, sugar, and a pinch of
salt. Let stand for 5 minutes until foamy. Add
softened butter and eggs, mixing until combined.

2. Flour Fantasia: Gradually add flour until a soft
dough forms, using the dough hook attachment on
low speed. Knead for 5-7 minutes, or until smooth
and elastic. Add a sprinkle of flour if the dough
feels too sticky.

3. Rise & Shine: Transfer the dough to a greased
bowl, cover tightly, and let rise in a warm place for
1-2 hours, or until doubled in size. Punch down the
dough to deflate it, then divide it into 3 equal pieces.

4. Braiding Beauty: Roll each piece of dough into a long rope. Pinch the ends together, then braid the dough, tucking the ends underneath. Place the braid on a greased baking sheet, cover loosely, and let rise for 30 minutes.

5. Golden Glow: Brush the braid with beaten egg wash and sprinkle with your favorite toppings (sesame seeds, poppy seeds, sugar!). Bake at 375°F (190°C) for 25-30 minutes, or until golden brown and fragrant. Let the braided masterpiece cool slightly on the baking sheet before slicing into it and revealing its tender, fluffy crumb.

Your kitchen will be filled with the aroma of success, and your guests will be singing your praises – a true baking triumph!

Bonus Tips for Bread Bonanza:

• **Warmth is key:** A warm environment allows yeast to thrive and helps your dough rise beautifully.

Use the oven's proofing setting or create a warm haven with a damp towel and a bowl of warm water.

• **Listen to your dough:** It's not just about measuring – feel the dough! If it feels sticky, add a bit more flour; if it's too dry, incorporate a splash of water.

• **Preheat with purpose:** Preheating your baking vessel, like a Dutch oven for sourdough, ensures a crisp crust and even baking.

• Experiment, adjust, enjoy! Don't be afraid to customize your bread. Add nuts, raisins, herbs, or spices to personalize your loaves. The possibilities are endless!

With these recipes and tips as your guide, your stand mixer will become your bread-making confidant. So, ditch the store-bought loaves, roll up your sleeves, and embark on your bread-baking adventure! Remember, practice makes perfect, and soon you'll be sharing crusty masterpieces that will leave everyone asking for seconds. Now go forth, unleash your inner artisan, and conquer the bread bonanza!

Pastry Panache

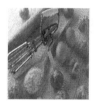

Stand mixer making pastry

Let's dive into the art of croissants, puff pastry, and éclairs, conquering techniques like lamination and chilling to create masterpieces that will leave everyone swooning. Buckle up, bakers, it's time to unleash your inner pastry pro!

Croissant Capers:

1. Dough Delight: In your mixer bowl, combine flour, yeast, sugar, salt, and warm milk. Use the dough hook attachment on low speed to form a shaggy dough. Increase speed to medium and knead for 5-7 minutes, or until smooth and elastic. Add a bit more flour if needed.

2. Chill Factor: Wrap the dough in plastic wrap and refrigerate for at least 2 hours, or overnight for best results. This gives the dough time to rest and develop its signature layers.

3. Butter Battle: Pound cold butter into a flat square on a lightly floured surface. Fold the dough around the butter, encasing it completely. This is the first of your "turns" - the key to building those gorgeous flaky layers.

4. Rolling Symphony: Roll the dough out into a rectangle, fold it into thirds, and give it another turn. Repeat this rolling and folding process 5-6 times, chilling the dough for 30 minutes between each turn. Patience is key here!

5. Shape & Rise: Shape the dough into crescents, tucking the ends underneath. Let them rise on a baking sheet for 1-2 hours, until doubled in size. Brush with egg wash and bake at 400°F (200°C) for 15-20 minutes, or until golden brown and puffed. The aroma of buttery heaven will fill your kitchen!

Puff Pastry Prowess:

1. Delicate Dough: Similar to the croissant dough, combine flour, salt, and water in your mixer. Knead on low speed until a smooth dough forms. Wrap it in plastic wrap and refrigerate for 30 minutes.

2. Butter Blitz: Roll out softened butter into a thin rectangle on a lightly floured surface. Place the dough rectangle on top of the butter, fold it into thirds, and roll it out again. This is your first "turn."

3. Rolling Rhythm: Repeat the rolling, folding, and chilling process 5-6 times, giving the dough a 30-minute rest between each turn. Each turn builds layer upon layer of buttery goodness.

4. Versatility Triumph: Use your puffed pastry masterpiece for savory pies, sweet turnovers, or decadent mille-feuille! Bake according to your desired recipe, reveling in the golden, flaky layers that melt in your mouth.

Éclair Elegance:

1. Choux Charisma: Mix water, butter, salt, and sugar in your mixer until the butter melts. Add flour all at once and mix on high speed until the dough pulls away from the sides and forms a ball. Let it cool slightly before adding eggs one at a time, mixing until incorporated.

2. Piping Perfection: Transfer the choux pastry dough to a piping bag fitted with a round tip. Pipe small mounds onto a lined baking sheet, keeping a space between them for puffing. Bake at 400°F (200°C) for 20-25 minutes, or until golden brown and puffed.

3. Creamy Conquering: Whip up your desired filling – pastry cream, chocolate ganache, or whipped cream are all wonderful options. Once the éclairs are cool, poke small holes on the bottom and pipe in your creamy delight. Dust with powdered sugar and voilà – miniature masterpieces ready to tantalize your taste buds!

Bonus Tips for Pastry Panache:

• **Chill time is crucial:** Lamination relies on alternating layers of cold butter and dough. Chilling prevents the butter from melting too quickly, creating those coveted flaky layers.

• **Sharp tools are your friends:** A sharp knife for shaping and a good piping bag are essential for precise pastry perfection.

• **Don't be afraid to experiment:** Get creative with fillings and toppings! Herbs, spices, and flavor extracts can add unexpected twists to your pastry creations.

• **Practice makes perfect:** Mastering laminated doughs takes time and patience. Don't get discouraged by a few misshapen pastries – celebrate the journey and enjoy the delicious discoveries along the way!

With these pastry pointers and your trusty stand mixer by your side, you'll soon be crafting flaky, feathery delights that will have everyone applauding your panache. So, preheat your oven, embrace the chill, and unleash your inner pastry artist! Remember, patience and practice are your guiding lights, and the rewards are pure pastry paradise! The light, airy texture and buttery layers of homemade croissants, the versatility of puff pastry that transforms into savory galettes or sweet danishes, and the elegant simplicity of an éclair filled with creamy perfection – these are the rewards that await your dedicated floury fingers.

So, don your apron, crank up your mixer, and embark on your pastry adventure! Remember, every fold, every chill, and every piping bag squeeze is a step closer to baking bliss. Now go forth, conquer the world of laminated doughs, and fill your kitchen (and your heart) with the magic of pastry panache!

I hope this extended ending provides a satisfying conclusion to your content. It emphasizes the delicious rewards of mastering pastry techniques and encourages readers to embrace the journey with enthusiasm and floury cheer. Please let me know if you have any other requests or need additional help!

Cake Captivation

Making cake with stand mixer

Let's soar beyond cupcakes and explore the majestic realm of complex cakes? Your trusty stand mixer awaits, eager to be your partner in crafting layered masterpieces, creamy cheesecakes, and impossibly light chiffon delights. Let's delve into the world of advanced techniques like egg separation and cake flour, transforming humble ingredients into skyscraping cakes that will steal the spotlight at any occasion. Prepare your whisks, bakers, it's time to ascend to Cake Olympus!

Layer Cake Majesty:

1. Egg-cellent Separation: Begin by separating your eggs. Use a clean bowl and gently crack each egg, separating the yolk from the white. A handy egg separator can be your yolk-taming ally. Trust me, stray yolks can spell doom for fluffy cakes!

2. Creamy Canvas: Beat softened butter and sugar in your stand mixer with the paddle attachment on medium speed until light and fluffy. This is the foundation of your cake's airiness, so take your time and let the mixer work its magic.

3. Yolk Parade: One at a time, add egg yolks to the creamed mixture, mixing on low until incorporated. Remember, patience is key – overmixing can lead to a dense cake.

4. Flour Fanfare: In a separate bowl, whisk together cake flour, baking powder, and salt. Gradually add this dry mixture to the wet ingredients in batches, alternating with milk or

buttermilk. Mix on low speed until just combined –
don't overmix!

5. Meringue Magic: In a clean bowl, whip the egg
whites to stiff peaks using the whisk attachment.
Start on low speed and gradually increase to high. A
pinch of cream of tartar can help stabilize the
meringue. Gently fold this airy cloud into the batter,
preserving its precious bubbles.

6. Baking Bonanza: Divide the batter evenly
between greased and floured cake pans. Bake at
350°F (175°C) for 25-30 minutes, or until a
toothpick inserted into the center comes out clean.
Let the cakes cool completely before frosting and
assembling your towering masterpiece.

Cheesecake Charisma:

1. Crust Symphony: Pulse graham crackers and
melted butter in a food processor until fine crumbs
form. Press the mixture into the bottom and sides of

a springform pan, creating a firm base for your creamy creation.

2. Creamy Dream Team: Beat softened cream cheese in your mixer with the paddle attachment until smooth and creamy. Gradually add sugar and mix until light and fluffy. Don't skimp on beating here – it ensures a silky-smooth cheesecake.

3. Egg-ceptional Addition: Add eggs one at a time, mixing on low until just incorporated. Scrape down the sides and bottom of the bowl to ensure everything gets mixed in. Overmixing can lead to cracks in your cheesecake, so be gentle!

4. Flavor Fusion: Stir in your desired flavorings – vanilla extract, lemon zest, or even melted chocolate are all delightful options. Gently fold in sour cream for added tang and richness.

5. Water Bath Wisdom: Wrap the springform pan tightly with foil to prevent water from seeping in. Place it in a larger pan filled with hot water, creating a water bath that ensures even baking and prevents cracks.

6. Baking Brilliance: Bake at 325°F (163°C) for 1-1.5 hours, or until the center is almost set but still slightly jiggly. Turn off the oven and let the cheesecake cool inside with the door slightly ajar. This prevents the cake from sinking. Chill overnight for the perfect creamy texture.

Chiffon Cloud Creations:

1. Flour Finesse: Sift cake flour several times to aerate it, creating the foundation for this impossibly light cake.

2. Egg White Whirlwind: Whip egg whites in your stand mixer with the whisk attachment on medium speed until foamy. Gradually add sugar until stiff peaks form. Patience is key here – this is what gives chiffon cakes their airy magic.

3. Egg Yolk Elegance: In a separate bowl, whisk egg yolks with the desired flavoring (vanilla, lemon zest, etc.) until thick and pale yellow. Gently fold this into the egg whites, taking care not to deflate the air.

4. Flour Fusion: Gently fold the sifted cake flour into the batter in batches, ensuring no lumps remain. This is a delicate dance – mix just until combined, or you'll lose the airiness.

5. Baking Bliss: Pour the batter into a tube pan ungreased (cake flour's magic!), and bake at 325°F (163°C) for 50-60 minutes, or until a toothpick inserted into the center comes out clean. In Inverted magic! To achieve that signature chiffon height, flip the pan upside down and let the cake cool completely while suspended on two bottles or cans –

gravity becomes your friend in this airy cake adventure! Once cool, run a knife around the edges of the pan and gently invert it onto a platter, revealing a cloud-like cake that will leave everyone speechless.

Bonus Tips for Cake Captivation:

• **Use quality ingredients:** Fresh eggs, real butter, and good-quality cake flour make a world of difference in flavor and texture.

• **Read recipe instructions carefully:** Baking relies on precise measurements and techniques. Pay attention to baking times, temperatures, and mixing instructions.

Don't overmix! This is the golden rule of cake baking. Overmixing leads to dense, tough cakes. Mix until just combined, then let your oven do the magic.

• **Embrace the chill:** Most cakes benefit from chilling the batter before baking. This allows the gluten in the flour to relax, resulting in a more tender crumb.

• **Frosting fun:** Get creative with your frosting! Experiment with flavors, textures, and colors to personalize your cake masterpieces.

With these recipes and tips as your guide, your stand mixer becomes your partner in cake-crafting excellence. So, crack those eggs, sift the flour, and unleash your inner cake artist! Remember, a little practice and a lot of enthusiasm go a long way. Now go forth, conquer the Cake Olympus, and let your creations speak for themselves – every bite a testament to your baking prowess!

Global Bake

Expand your baking horizons beyond familiar shores. Your trusty stand mixer is your passport to a world of international flavors and textures! Let's embark on a delicious journey, tackling iconic treats like Italian biscotti, French macarons, and German stollen, all adapted for the ease and precision of your kitchen companion. Get your oven hot and your whisk prepped, globetrotting bakers, it's time to conquer the world, one bite at a time!

Italian Biscotti Bliss:

1. Almond Delight: Pulse almonds, walnuts, and hazelnuts in a food processor until finely chopped. In your stand mixer with the paddle attachment, combine chopped nuts, sugar, zest of an orange and lemon, and flour. Add eggs one at a time, mixing until just incorporated. Don't overmix – a slightly sticky dough is key for crispy biscotti.

2. Shaping Symphony: Divide the dough in half and form each half into a thick log on a baking sheet lined with parchment paper. Brush with beaten egg white and sprinkle with additional nuts or sugar for a touch of sweetness.

3. Twice-Baked Brilliance: Bake at 325°F (163°C) for 30 minutes. Cut the logs diagonally into 1-inch slices while still warm. Arrange them cut-side down on the baking sheet and bake for another 15-20 minutes, or until golden brown and crisp. Savor these crunchy delights dipped in coffee, wine, or simply enjoyed on their own.

French Macaron Magic:

1. Almond Flour Finesse: Grind almonds into a fine flour in your food processor. Sift it with powdered sugar in a bowl, removing any lumps for that smooth macaron shell.

2. Meringue Maestro: In your stand mixer with the whisk attachment, whip egg whites to soft peaks. Gradually add sugar until stiff peaks form, creating a glossy, stable meringue. Gently fold in the almond flour mixture until just combined, preserving the air bubbles.

3. Piping Perfection: Transfer the batter to a piping bag fitted with a round tip. Pipe small dollops onto baking sheets lined with parchment paper, leaving space for spreading. Tap the baking sheet to remove air bubbles and let the macarons rest for 30 minutes to form a skin.

• **Baking Bonanza:** Bake at 300°F (150°C) for 15-20 minutes, or until the shells are firm and slightly cracked. Let them cool completely before filling with your favorite ganache, buttercream, or jam. These delicate, colorful cookies are a true Parisian treat!

German Stollen Grandeur:

1. Soaked Fruit Symphony: Mix raisins, dried cranberries, and apricots with rum or orange juice, and let them soak overnight for plumpness and flavor.

2. Nutty Dough Delight: In your stand mixer with the dough hook attachment, combine flour, yeast, sugar, spices like cardamom and cinnamon, and warm milk. Knead until smooth and elastic, then add softened butter and knead until incorporated. Let the dough rise in a warm place until doubled in size.

3. Fruit & Nut Fusion: Gently knead the soaked fruit and ground nuts into the risen dough. Shape the dough into a long oval loaf and tuck the ends underneath. Place it on a greased baking sheet, seam-side down, and let rise again for an hour.

4. Buttery Blanket: Brush the stollen with melted butter and sprinkle with sugar and almond slivers. Bake at 350°F (175°C) for about 1 hour, or until golden brown and an internal temperature of 190°F (88°C) is reached. Wrap the stollen in foil while still warm, then in a clean kitchen towel, and let it rest overnight for the flavors to meld. This dense, fruity bread is a Christmastime tradition, but delicious all year round!

Bonus Tips for Global Bakes:

• **Research your recipes:** Each culture has its own twists and techniques. Dive into the history and nuances of each treat to truly understand its essence.

• **Adapt ingredients:** Not all ingredients are readily available everywhere. Find locally sourced substitutes or adjust quantities to suit your taste and pantry.

- **Embrace imperfections:** These international bakes may require more practice than familiar cookies. Don't be discouraged by a few mishaps – celebrate the journey and the unique flavors you're creating!

- **Share your creations:** Gather friends and family around your global baking bounty. Sharing the experience adds to the joy of discovering new taste sensations.

With your stand mixer by your side and a spirit of adventure in your heart, you can conquer the world, one delicious bite at a time! So, preheat your oven, crank up your mixer, and embark on a culinary voyage unlike any other.

From crunchy Italian biscotti to delicate French macarons and rich German stollen, your kitchen becomes a global bakery, filled with the aroma of distant lands and the joy of shared experiences.

Remember, baking is more than just following recipes; it's about exploring new cultures, experimenting with flavors, and creating memories that will last a lifetime. So, gather your ingredients, your loved ones, and your insatiable curiosity – the world of international baking awaits, and your trusty stand mixer is your passport to endless delicious adventures!

Part 4: Beyond the Basics

Decoration Divas

Rainbow Sprinkle Funfetti Cake

So, you've mastered the art of fluffy cakes and gooey brownies – now it's time to transform them into masterpieces! Buckle up, bakers, because we're diving into the dazzling world of cake decorating! No fancy piping bags or professional skills required, just a dab of creativity, a sprinkle of enthusiasm, and your trusty spatula are all you need to become a Decoration Diva. Get ready to turn those humble cakes into stunning showstoppers and unleash your inner cake artist!

Frosting Finesse:

• **Creamy Canvas:** Start with your favorite frosting – buttercream, cream cheese, ganache – perfectly whipped and ready to embrace its destiny. Grab a palette knife or offset spatula – your trusty tools for frosting mastery.

• **Smooth Sailing:** Spread a generous layer of frosting over your cooled cake like a painter coating their canvas. Work from the top down, using a circular motion to achieve that smooth, professional finish. Don't worry about perfection – embrace the natural swirls and textures!

• **Crumb Catcher:** For a flawless final touch, chill your frosted cake for 30 minutes. This sets the frosting and allows you to gently sweep away any stray crumbs for a polished presentation.

Piping Perfection:

- **Bag of Tricks:** Invest in a basic piping bag fitted with a round tip – your gateway to piped borders and whimsical decorations. Fill it with a contrasting frosting color for eye-catching designs.

- **Borderline Brilliant:** Pipe a simple border around the base of your cake, or get adventurous with scallops, zigzags, or even dots! Practice makes perfect, so don't be afraid to experiment on parchment paper before adorning your masterpiece.

- **Message Maestro:** Want to write a birthday wish or a fun slogan? Fill a small piping bag with frosting and use a fine tip to write your message directly onto the cake. Think of it as edible calligraphy!

Sprinkle Sensation:

- **Rainbow Rain:** Let your personality shine through with a vibrant sprinkle shower! Choose sprinkles that match your theme, favorite colors, or even the occasion. Chopped nuts, dried fruit, and mini candies can also add exciting textures and flavors.

• **Strategic Sprinkles:** Don't just dump them on! Create patterns, borders, or even write with sprinkles for a unique touch. Use stencils or templates for fun shapes, or let your creativity guide your sprinkle placement.

• **Less is More:** Remember, sometimes less is more. A few strategically placed sprinkles can add just the right amount of sparkle and elegance, like edible jewels crowning your creation.

Bonus Tips for Decoration Divas:
• **Embrace imperfection:** Your cake doesn't have to be competition-worthy. Imperfections add charm and character – nobody sees them better than you do, anyway!

- **Make it personal:** Use colors, flavors, and decorations that reflect your personality or the occasion. It's your cake canvas, so let your creativity flow!

Practice makes perfect: Don't be discouraged if your first piped border isn't a masterpiece. Keep practicing, and soon you'll be piping like a pro!

Have fun! This is all about enjoying the process and expressing yourself through cake. Put on your apron, crank up the music, and let your inner diva shine!

So, ditch the store-bought cakes and embrace the joy of DIY decorating! With these simple techniques and a sprinkle of imagination, you'll be transforming ordinary cakes into extraordinary creations in no time.

Remember, practice makes perfect, but even the messiest masterpiece is born from the joy of creation. So, grab your frosting, channel your inner artist, and unleash your Decoration Diva magic! The world (and your cake stand) awaits!

Troubleshooting Toolbox

Ever pulled a sunken cake from the oven or watched cookies spread into oblivion? Don't fret, bakers! We've all been there, but fear not, for this trusty toolbox holds the solutions to your baking woes. With a sprinkle of knowledge and a dash of preventative measures, you'll be mastering every step from measuring to munching in no time!

Cake Calamities: Solution & Prevention

• **Sunken Surprise:** Did your cake cave in like a deflated soufflé? Blame an overworked batter, too much leavening, or an uneven oven temperature.
Solution: Gently fold ingredients instead of beating, double-check baking powder amounts, and invest in an oven thermometer.

Prevention: Avoid overmixing, measure precisely, and preheat your oven accurately.

• **Dense Disappointment:** A heavy, brick-like cake can be caused by too much flour, not enough leavening, or overbaking.

Solution: Use the scoop-and-level method for flour, double-check baking soda/powder amounts, and reduce baking time if needed.

Prevention: Measure flour correctly, ensure correct leavening agents, and keep an eye on the timer.

• **Burnt Bonfire:** Is your cake more charcoal than cocoa? Blame excessive oven temperature, a dark baking pan, or overbaking.

Solution: Adjust oven temperature to recipe specifications, switch to a lighter pan, and reduce baking time if needed.

Prevention: Check your oven's temperature, choose a light-colored pan, and set timers and alarms.

Cookie Catastrophes:

• **Flatline Flops:** Did your cookies spread into sad puddles? Blame too much liquid, too little flour, or improper chilling. **Solution:** Double-check recipe measurements, add a bit more flour, and consider chilling the dough before baking. **Prevention:** Measure liquids accurately, adjust flour to desired consistency, and chill dough for at least 30 minutes for better shaping.

• **Cratered Calamity:** Are your cookies riddled with cracks and craters? Blame too much baking powder, uneven heat, or opening the oven during baking.

Solution: Reduce baking powder slightly, ensure even oven temperature, and resist the urge to peek!

Prevention: Use fresh baking powder, preheat the oven properly, and avoid peeking for the first 10 minutes of baking.

• **Pale & Pasty:** Did your cookies emerge pale and unappetizing? Blame underbaking, low oven temperature, or too much sugar.

Solution: Increase baking time slightly, adjust oven temperature if needed, and consider reducing sugar for a deeper color. **Prevention:** Keep an eye on baking time, check oven temperature accuracy, and adjust sugar based on desired color and texture.

Bonus Toolbox Tips:

• **Freshness First:** Use fresh ingredients for optimal results. Expired baking powder or stale flour can significantly impact your bakes.

• **Temperature Tango:** Ensure your oven temperature is accurate. Invest in an oven thermometer and preheat properly for even baking.

• **Read & Re-read:** Don't just skim the recipe! Understanding instructions and ingredient roles can prevent common mistakes.

• **Measure with precision:** Accurate measurements are crucial for successful baking. Invest in good measuring tools and avoid eyeballing ingredients.

• **Practice makes progress:** Baking is a learning journey. Don't get discouraged by occasional mishaps. Embrace the process, keep practicing, and soon you'll be wowing everyone with your baking prowess!

Remember, bakers, these are just common baking blunders and their solutions. Every recipe and situation is unique, so don't be afraid to experiment, adjust, and most importantly, have fun in the kitchen! With your trusty toolbox and a dash of baking bravery, you'll conquer any culinary challenge and emerge victorious with delectable delights. So, preheat your oven, dust off your apron, and get ready to bake!

Glossary of Baking Terms

Ingredients:

• **Baking powder & Baking soda:** Leavening agents, these bubbly buddies help our bakes rise like fluffy clouds. Baking powder is a complete leavening system, while baking soda needs an acidic ingredient like buttermilk to activate.

• **Cake flour:** A finely milled flour with low protein content, it creates tender, delicate cakes. Think feather-light chiffon and melt-in-your-mouth crumbles.

• **Cream:** Butter whipped with sugar until light and fluffy, it adds richness, moisture, and air to cakes and frostings. Think creamy cheesecake fillings and buttery cookie dough.

• **Egg whites & Yolks:** Separating these sunshine stars unlocks a world of possibilities! Whites whip into airy meringues for mousses and macarons, while yolks add richness and color to custards and pasta.

• **Flour (All-purpose, Bread, etc.):** The backbone of baking, flour provides structure and texture. All-purpose works well for a variety of bakes, while bread flour, with its higher protein content, creates chewy crusts and hearty loaves.

• **Milk & buttermilk:** Liquid heroes, they add moisture, activate leavening agents, and influence texture. Buttermilk adds a tangy twist to pancakes and cakes, while milk provides a neutral base for cookies and pies.

• **Sugar:** Our sweet friend comes in many forms, each with its own personality. Granulated sugar sweetens and adds structure, while powdered sugar makes delicate frostings and icings. Brown sugar adds moisture and complex flavors to cookies and cakes.

• **Yeast:** This living microorganism eats sugar and releases carbon dioxide, making doughs rise like puffy pillows. Perfect for breads, pizzas, and cinnamon rolls!

Techniques:

• **Bloom:** Soaking dry ingredients in liquid to soften them and achieve a smooth texture. Think gelatin blooming in cold water for creamy panna cotta.

• **Creaming:** Beating butter and sugar together until light and fluffy, incorporating air for a tender crumb. Imagine fluffy buttercream and melt-in-your-mouth cookies.

• **Folding:** Gently incorporating dry ingredients into wet ingredients with a cutting and lifting motion, preserving air bubbles for a light and airy result. Think chiffon cakes and soufflés.

• **Kneading:** Working dough with your hands or a mixer to develop the gluten network, creating structure and elasticity. Imagine kneading pizza dough until smooth and stretchy.

• **Proofing:** Allowing yeast dough to rest in a warm place to rise and double in size. Think doughy clouds forming in your bread bowl before baking.

• **Sifting:** Passing dry ingredients through a sieve to remove lumps and aerate them for a lighter texture. Think fluffy pancakes and airy cakes.

• **Whipping:** Beating egg whites or cream with air until stiff peaks form, incorporating air for volume and stability. Think dreamy meringues and silky whipped cream.

Bonus Goodies:

• **Bain-marie:** A water bath, gently heating delicate desserts like custards and cheesecakes without scorching. Think luxurious pots de crème and smooth cheesecake fillings.

• **Piping:** Using a bag with a tip to decorate with frosting, create borders, write messages, or add intricate designs. Think piped borders on cupcakes and delicate cake decorations.

• **Tempering:** Gently melting chocolate to a specific temperature for a smooth, shiny finish and preventing seizing. Think glossy chocolate ganache and decadent truffles.

Fun Facts:

• Did you know the first stand mixer was invented in 1908 and weighed a whopping 80 quarts? It was designed for commercial bakeries to tackle heavy loads of bread dough! Thankfully, today's mixers are much smaller and easier to manage, even for the home baker.

• The oldest working KitchenAid mixer on record is over 90 years old! It's a testament to the quality and durability of these amazing kitchen appliances.

• More Than Mixing: Your stand mixer isn't just for cakes and cookies! With additional attachments, you can grind meat, make pasta, churn ice cream, whip up mashed potatoes, and even stuff sausages. It's like a kitchen superhero with multiple superpowers!

Conclusion

And so, the oven light dims on this baking adventure, but the warmth of creativity remains. Thank you, fellow bakers, for joining me on this journey of flour, sugar, and endless possibilities. Remember, the true magic lies not in picture-perfect pastries, but in the joy of learning, experimenting, and sharing sweet creations. Keep practicing, keep exploring, and never let your oven grow cold. Happy baking, and may your kitchens be filled with laughter and delicious triumphs!

Made in the USA
Middletown, DE
10 January 2024

47602046R00049